HUDSON AREA LIBRARY

SLOWINSKI

DIRECT ART BOOKS

Introduction by
Andrei Codrescu

Centerpiece by
Dakota Lane

Epilogue by
Mike Feder

Front cover:
Breakfast Party

Back cover:
Drive to The Country

End pages:
Sketchbook Pages

Frontispiece:
Exploding Head

This Page:
Detail from Going Shopping

Editor and Publisher: Paul Winslow
Assistant Editor: Marlene Robinson
Art and Design: T. P. Lowens

Published in the United States of America in 2003 by Direct Art Books. All rights reserved. No part of the contents of this book may be reproduced by any means in any original or altered form without the written permission of the Publisher. Direct any inquiries to:

Direct Art Books
PO Box 503
Phoenicia, NY 12464

directartbooks@aol.com
http://www.directart.org

Printed and bound in China

ISBN 0-9742506-0-0

CONTENTS

SLOWINSKILAND
by Andrei Codrescu
7

THE EARLY WORK: HOW IT ALL BEGAN
by Robert Smythe
8

CARNIVAL OF SUBURBIA
24

FAMILY AND CHILDREN
38

URBAN VIEWS
52

THE FATTIES
56

BUSINESS AND FINANCE
68

FIRE AND BRIMSTONE
80

AN EMPIRE OF UNENDING HORROR - BUT FUNNY
by Dakota Lane
104

CREATION AND EVOLUTION
106

ANIMALS AND FARM
110

FOOD
122

CLOWNS AND FREAKS
134

ROGUE HEADS
138

PARTIES AND POLITICS
146

CULTURAL ICONS
158

CONSUMERISM
166

DOCTORS AND NURSES
174

INDUSTRIAL NIGHTMARE
180

RESTORING THE ESSENTIAL GOODNESS
by Mike Feder
187

A portrait of the artist Slowinski, taken by the Japanese photographer Hisashi at Limner Gallery, October 2002.

SLOWINSKI

b.1957

SLOWINSKILAND

By Andrei Codrescu

The country of Slowinski is bordered by the satirical principality of Daumier, the futuristic industrial park of Ferdinand Leger, Orwell's Animal Farm, and several territories ruled by dark princelings such as George Grosz and Stanislaw Lem. All these dangerous art zones have embassies in Slowinskiland. For instance, Daumier's acid commentaries on the French bourgeoisie are echoed in Slowinski's agitprop politics; Ferdinand Leger's futuristic vision of a world that is almost all machine is part of the Slowinskiland constitution; Orwell's Animal Farm with its menagerie of terror and its soundtrack of pain provides the foodstuffs; George Grosz' Dada nausea for the sickly obesity of overconsumption and war-lust finds a place of honor in Slowinskiland pedagogy; the dark Polish Futurism of Stanislaw Lem describes the very landscape.

Slowinski's country is not a tourist destination. In fact, the very idea of "tourism" is repellent. One imagines a group of Disney-bound holiday goers being devoured like dog-chops or worm-burgers before they even reach the first rest stop. In fact, there are no rest stops. Looking at the organically monstrous creatures of his world one feels the anxiety of someone who strayed by mistake into Hieronymous Bosch's hell. A diseased white lecher embraces a degraded black female while they both suck poison from barrels attached to their bodies. A fat baby diapered and armed like John Wayne postures before a TV spewing blood, while a tiny lynched figure completes the décor of a motel room that makes the Bates Motel look idyllic by comparison. A grocery cart with a human head shoves down the isle of a market laden with menacingly heavy goods. Every item on the store shelf is politically explosive. A human-headed hydra feeds orgiastically on its own flesh. A grotesque couple strolls down the street in a seemingly peaceful suburb: she is a dog-headed, cigarette-smoking, pregnant abomination while her four-legged partner drags along a scary, fat head whose eyes are filled with horror.

What makes Slowinskiland so uncompromisingly frightening is its perverse familiarity. The inhabitants may be monsters, but they are only the dark aspects of people familiar to us. The land may be bubbling with carnal distress but it's a land we know, it's America, Slowinski's America. The rhetoric of the allegories is also familiar. When I was growing up in communist Romania, the anti-capitalist rhetoric we learned in school was inhabited by a vast menagerie: we had "capitalist pigs," "hydra-headed corporations," "bourgeois hyenas," "imperialist dogs," and many more. In some way, this rhetoric was unfair to animals, and I always thought that people were a lot more loathsome than those beasts. In its simple, vicious way, commie ranting was still beholden to the ethnocentric tradition of the bourgeois Enlightenment. But if such polemical echoes haunt Slowinskiland, they have become a lot more sophisticated, because it's much later in history. Since those somewhat innocent days of 50s Stalinism, we've experienced horrors that have found many different expressions in Surrealistic and gothic art. These too have found a genial host in Slowinskiland.

On the other hand, Slowinski is a moral rabble-rouser who yields prophetic simplicity. He points out our vices in nearly medieval, scholastic order. Greed, gluttony, stupidity, and lust, all come under the scrutiny of bright lights. There is a punctilious and skilled attention to detail here for those fearless enough to venture within. You cannot leave Slowinskiland off your map if you want to see the whole picture of our world now in all its dimensions.

ANDREI CODRESCU
Editor of "Exquisite Corpse, a Journal of Life & Letters"

http://www.codrescu.com
http://www.corpse.org

The Early Work: How It All Began
by Robert Smythe

Figure 1, Portrait, Oil, 32" x 20", 1976

Figure 3, Winter Breath (detail), Oil, 42" x 60", 1981

The images in this book represent a series of work created by Slowinski during the years 1984 - 2003. Prior to 1984, the artist worked in several distinctive yet very different styles. The earliest pieces (1975-77, fig. 1) were characterized by an expressionist application and dark earth toned pigments, representing the earth as an elemental part of humanity. His early work was purely emotional, the figures expressing states of anguish and suffering. These paintings evolved to incorporate a photographic based design (1977-78, fig. 2). Influenced in part by the photo-realist painters popularized in the 1960s and 1970s, the work evolved further to incorporate a heightened level of graphic realism (1979-82, fig. 3). This series retains strong emotive content, enhanced through the use of altered coloration. Focused sharply on patterns of light and shade, Slowinski broke down areas within each painting into geometric shapes, which were chromatically toned using a numeric system.

During 1983 Slowinski became frustrated with the limitations of reality-based imagery. He felt that every style and technique of figurative painting had already been perfected, with "the only remaining frontier to be explored is the one inside the mind." Using this concept as the basis for his work, he embarked on a new series of paintings that would come only from the imagination, abandoning the use of elements from the external world.

The concept was fixed, but Slowinski had no idea what he would paint. A blank canvas was stretched and placed in the studio. It sat empty on the easel. A day went by, then weeks passed. As time went on the artist became despondent. Of this time the artist said, "I felt my mind was empty and I had nothing to say."

One afternoon something took hold as, "a strange feeling suddenly possessed me and I picked up the brush." Moments later a large head was drawn on the canvas. A character appeared to emerge from the lines on its own; it was the figure of a grotesque, green-eyed, wealthy heiress. Completing this painting another canvas was stretched and the process repeated, then another. Each time a new figure emerged, an egg headed politician, a fat businessman, a psychiatrist, a pig farmer and others. These initial characters, depicted in the first section of the book, formed the conceptual base for the paintings that were to come. The categories of paintings in the following chapters grew out of these original characters, as if from each invented personality an extended family was born.

The works are not depicted sequentially as there was no order based on subject. As the artist's mind drifted from idea to idea so did his paintings and the subjects varied seemingly at random, but to the original concept Slowinski held true. He would paint the world around him not as he saw it, but only as it affected him and as he remembered it to be.

Figure 2, The Visitor, Oil, 74" x 84", 1978

BIG BUSINESSMAN IN HARLEM   Acrylic on canvas   60" x 52"   1985   Collection Richard Golub

TWO RICH KIDS   Acrylic on canvas   42" x 56"   1984   Collection Michael Clifford

MR. MINSTER   Acrylic on canvas   56" x 42"   1984   Collection Robert F White

BART BIGGY- POLITICIAN   Acrylic on canvas   56" x 42"   1984   Collection Richard Golub

DOCTOR LOBOTO   Acrylic on canvas   56" x 42"   1984   Collection Richard Golub

PIG FARMER   Acrylic on canvas   56" x 42"   1985   Collection Richard Golub

COUSIN NICK Acrylic on canvas 56" x 42" 1984 Collection of the artist

HEAD OF INDUSTRY #1   Acrylic on canvas   56" x 42"   1985   Collection Richard Golub

HEAD OF INDUSTRY #2   Acrylic on canvas   60" x 48"   1985   Collection Richard Golub

INDUSTRIOUS PIG   Acrylic on canvas   34" x 46"   1984   Collection Anastasia Winslow

BURGER BOOTH   Acrylic on canvas   54" x 72"   1985   Collection ACA Gallery

EGG FACTORY   Acrylic on canvas   34" x 46"   1984   Collection Jerry Kaufmann

RUSH HOUR   Acrylic on canvas   56" x 62"   1985   Collection Sylvia Stept

TV MAN   Acrylic on canvas   42" x 36"   1985   Collection John Minden

NEIGHBORHOOD WATCH   Acrylic on canvas   56" x 72"   1986   Collection Richard Golub

BLOCKHEADS   Acrylic on canvas   84" x 68"   1986   Collection Jorge Letelier Yavar

The Carnival of Suburbia

THE CARNIVAL OF SUBURBIA   Acrylic on canvas   78" x 68"   1988   Collection of the artist

DRITE TO THE COUNTRY   Acrylic on canvas   68" x 48"   1990   Collection Barry Goodman

RIDE THROUGH TOWN   Acrylic on canvas   68" x 72"   1991   Collection of the artist

DOG LICK   Acrylic on canvas   12" x 24"   2001   Collection Andrei Codrescu

NOSEY NEIGHBOR   Acrylic on canvas   16" x 10"   1989   Estate of Berrien Thorne Fregos

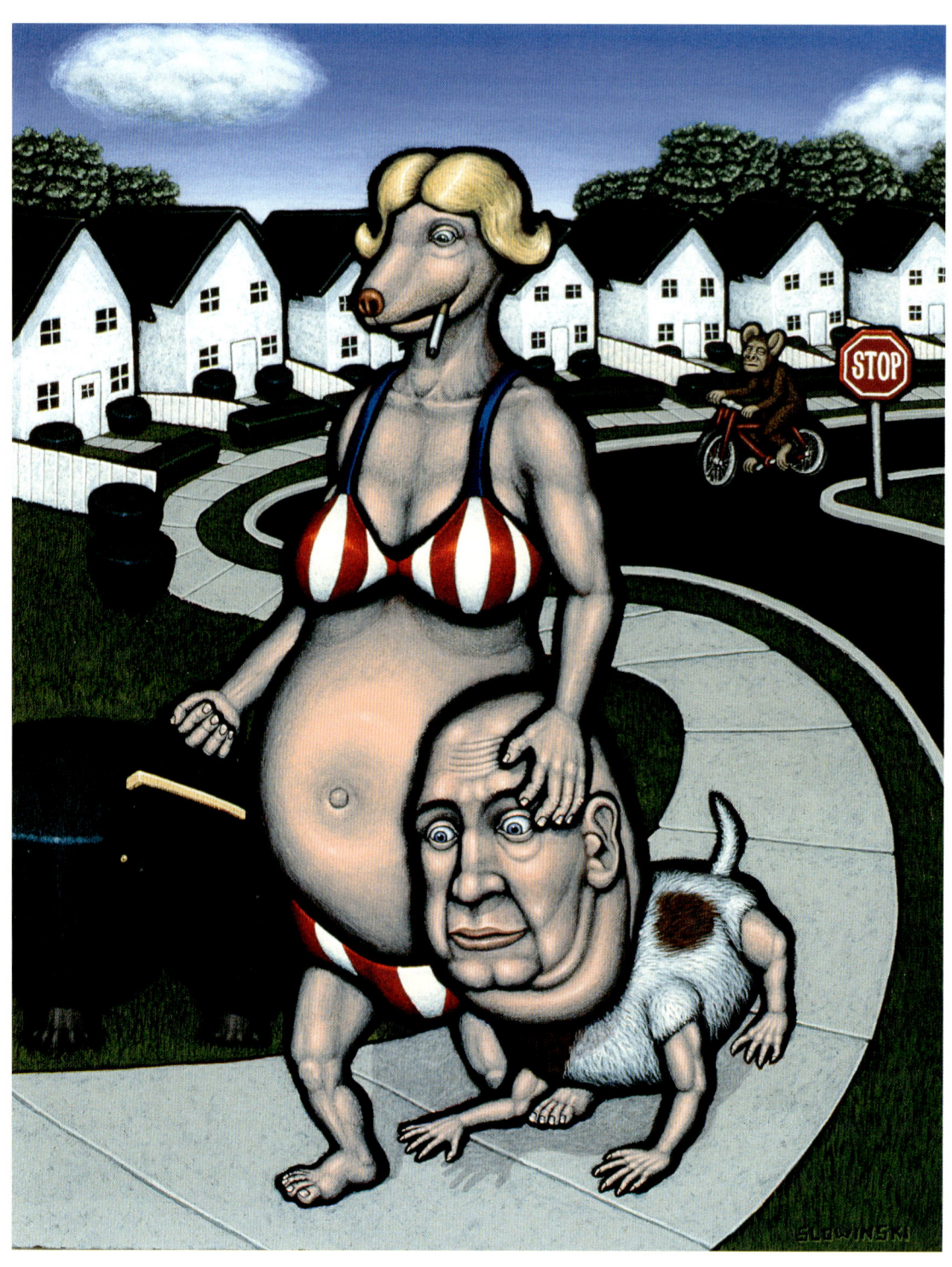

THE HAPPY COUPLE   Acrylic on canvas   20" x 16"   2000   Collection of the artist

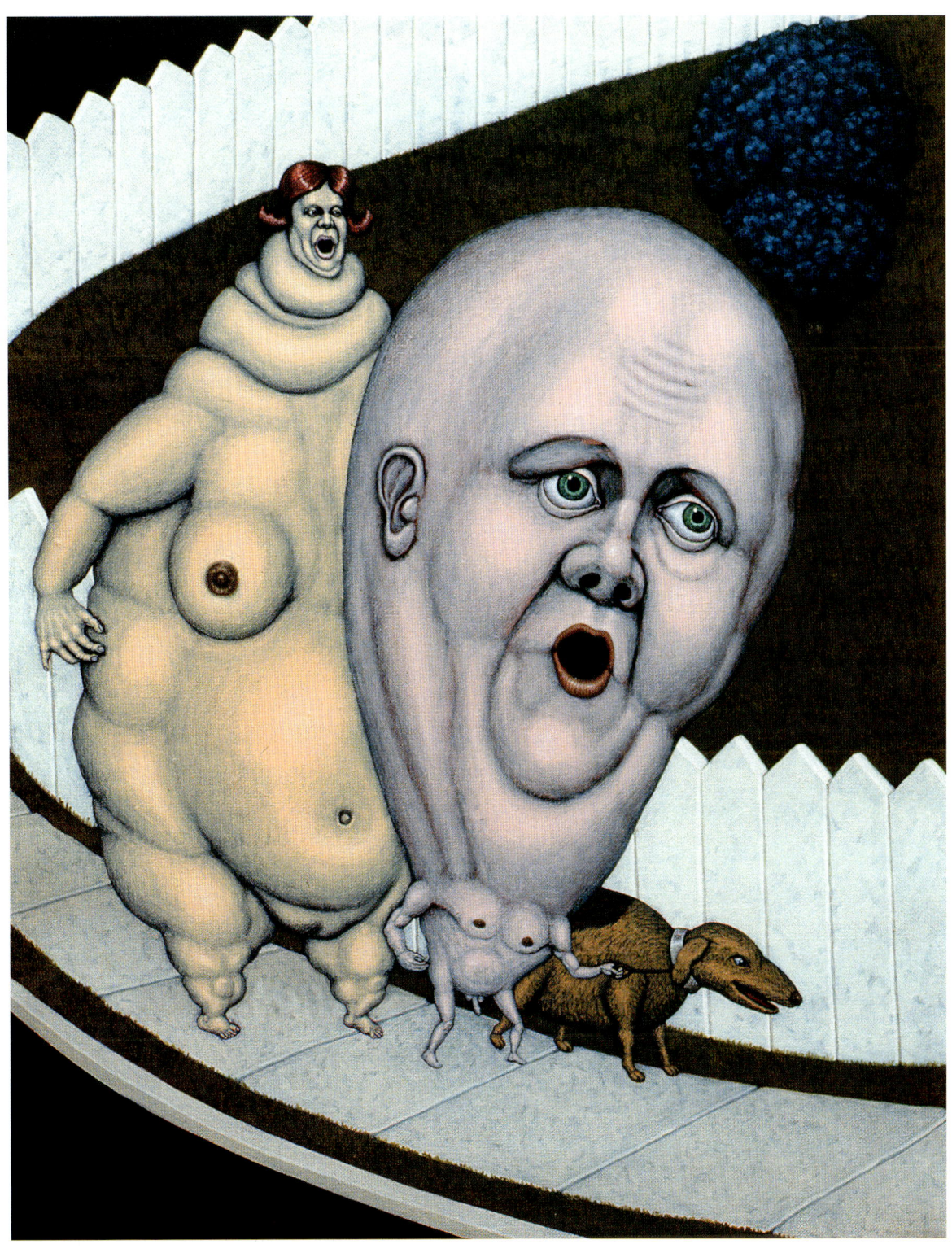

PERFECT COUPLE   Acrylic on canvas   18" x 14"   1992   Collection Christopher Castroviejo

GRANNY   Acrylic on canvas   10" x 12"   1988   Collection Richard Golub

MR. BLOCKHEAD   Acrylic on canvas   38" x 32"   1987   Collection of the artist

SMOKEFACES   Acrylic on canvas   20" x 10"   1994   Collection Dr. Daryl Isaacs

GRANNY PORTRAIT   Acrylic on canvas   10" x 8"   1999   Collection of the artist

BIRD BRAIN   Acrylic on canvas   45" x 34"   1990   Collection Richard Golub

DISASTER Acrylic on canvas 20" x 16" 1992 Collection Laura Golder

FAMILY DINNER   Acrylic on canvas   78" x 64"   1986   Collection of the artist

Family and Children

BUY-MOR MART   Acrylic on canvas   72" x 54"   1987   Collection Kenneth Silva

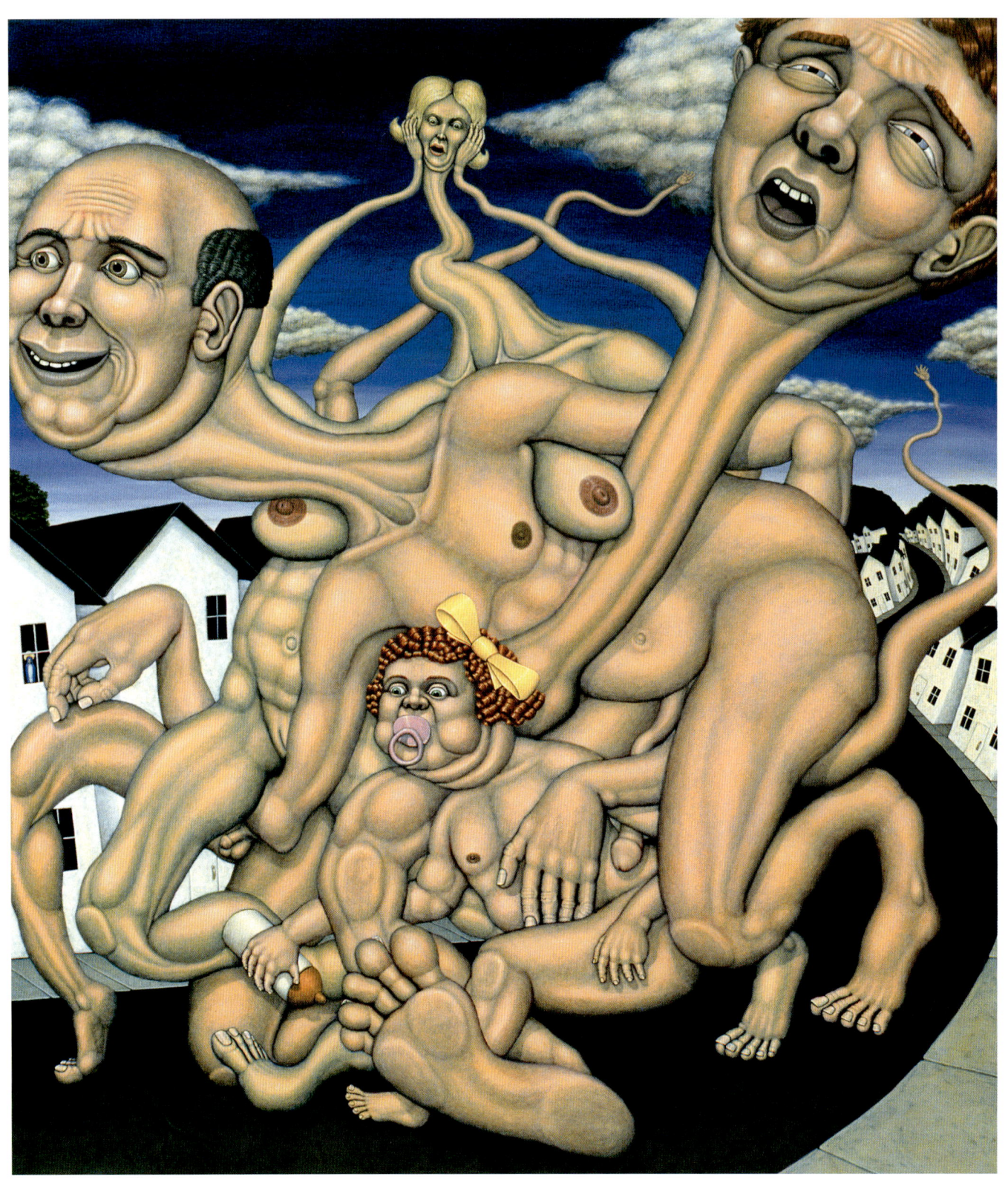

DYSFUNCTIONAL FAMILY   Acrylic on canvas   72" x 64"   1992   Collection Barry Goodman

TRIP TO THE MAILBOX   Acrylic on canvas   94" x 58"   1993   Collection of the artist

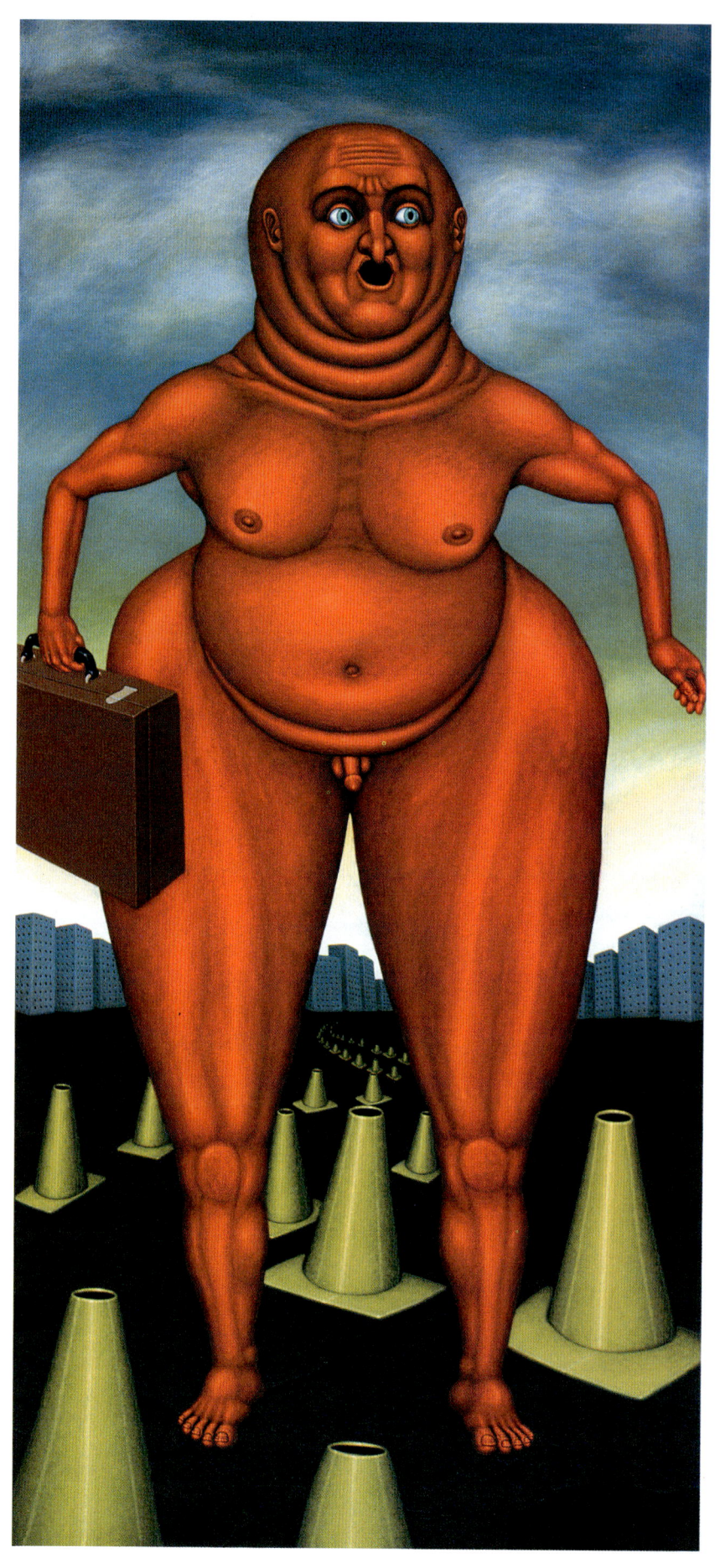

GOING TO WORK (PSYCHEDELIC FAMILY, FATHER)
Acrylic on canvas 90" x 42" 1993 Collection of the artist

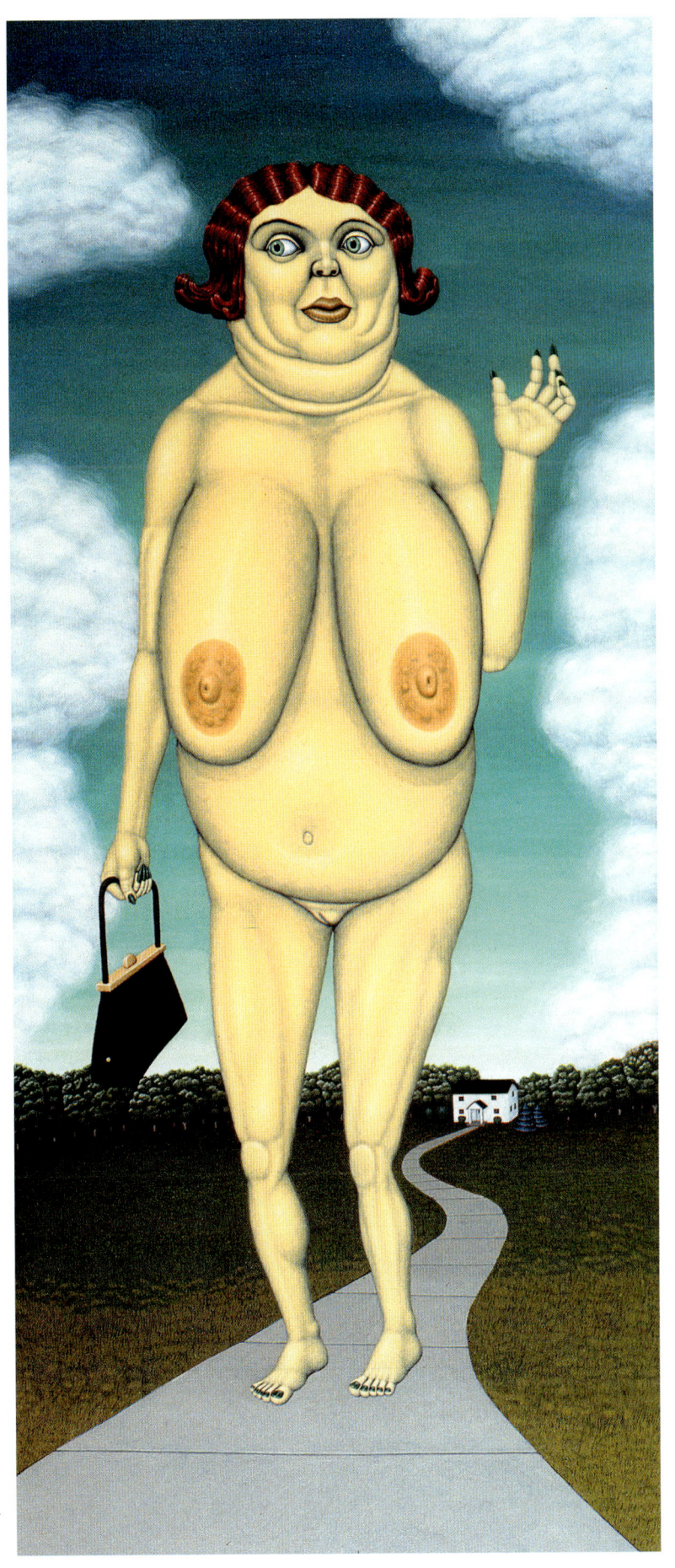

GOING SHOPPING (PSYCHEDELIC FAMILY, MOTHER)
Acrylic on canvas   80" x 34"   1993   Collection of the artist

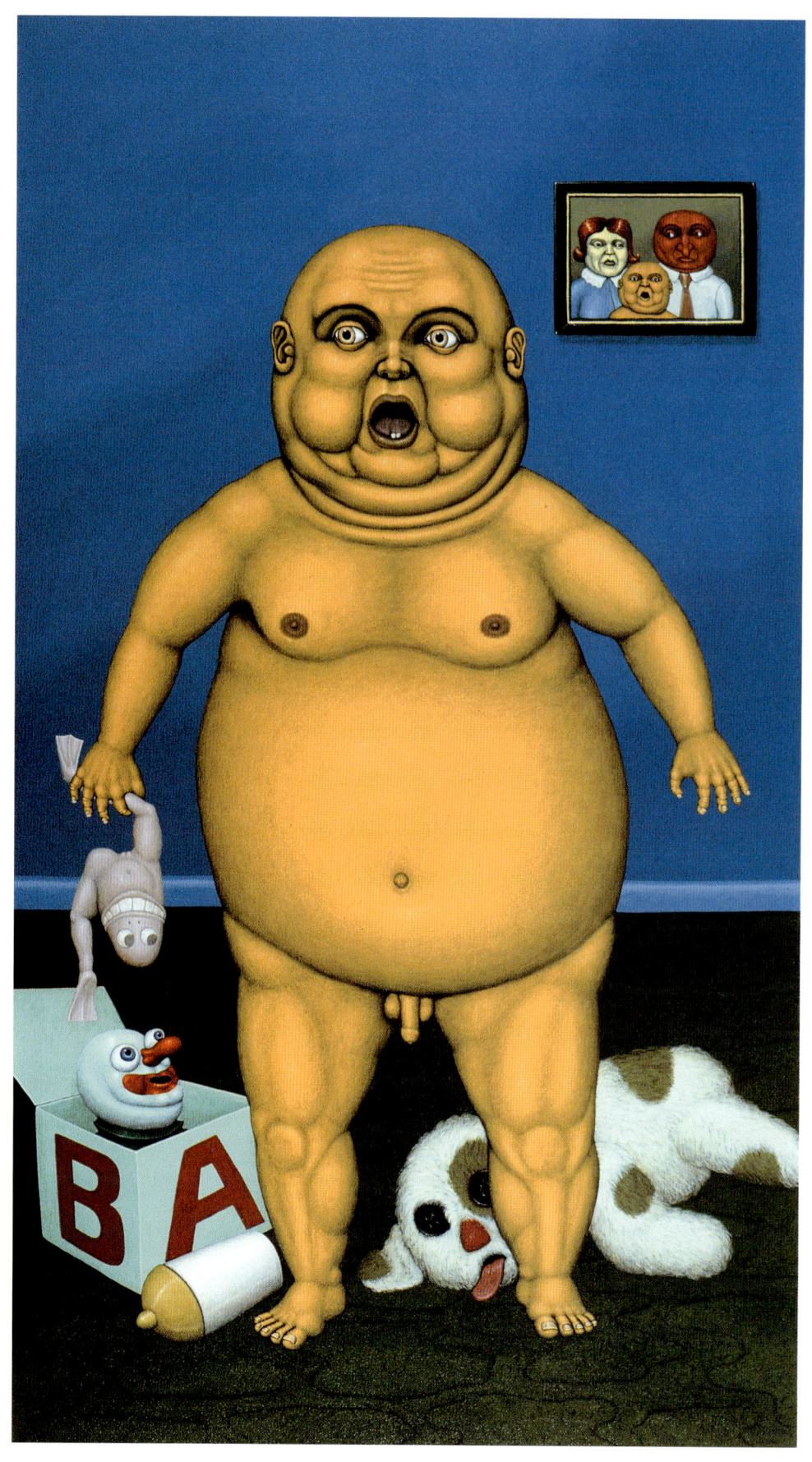

BABY (PSYCHEDELIC FAMILY, BABY)
Acrylic on canvas   60" x 34"   1993   Collection Barry Goodman

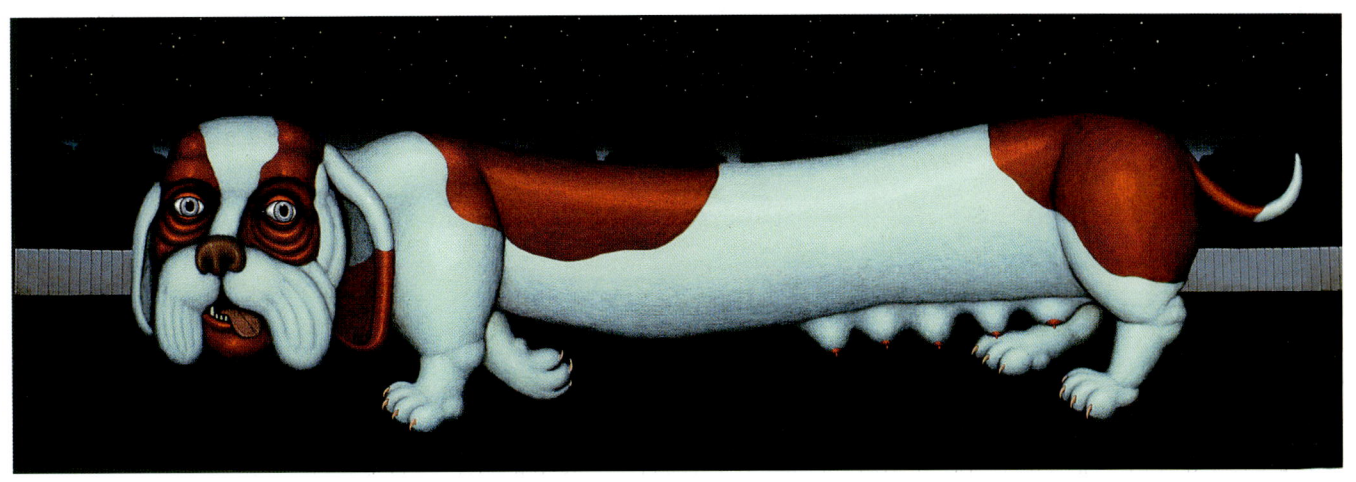

THE DOG (PSYCHEDELIC FAMILY, PET)
Acrylic on canvas   20" x 52"   1993   Collection Richard Golub

THE PSYCHEDELIC FAMILY

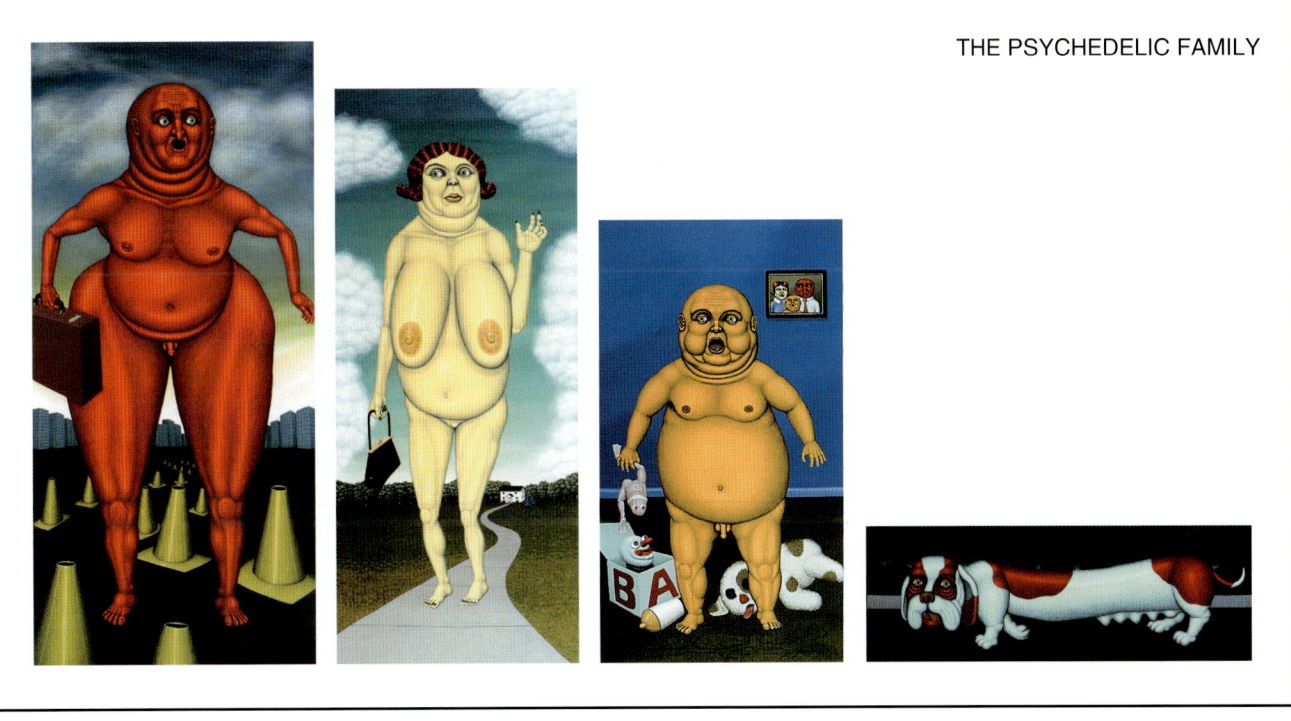

45

CRA--ZEE CLOWN   Acrylic on canvas   20" x 24"   2002   Collection Brett Oppenheimer

POST 911 BABY   Acrylic on canvas   56" x 42"   2002   Collection Barry Goodman

BOY WITH BREAKFAST   Acrylic on canvas   18" x 14"   1991   Collection David Andrews

Left: BREAKFAST PARTY   Acrylic on canvas   78" x 64"   1990   Collection Estate of Ted Churchill

BABY WITH TV DINNER   Acrylic on canvas   18" x 14"   1989   Collection Zyfryd Dabrowski

CHRISTMAS Acrylic on canvas 52" x 56" 1990 Collection David Ehrlich

CITY ON FIRE   Pencil   4" x 6"   1992   Collection of the artist

Urban Views

DRUG FREE ZONE   Acrylic on canvas   68" x 84"   1988   Collection Laura Golder

CRACK HEAD   Acrylic on canvas   10" x 8"   1994   Private collection

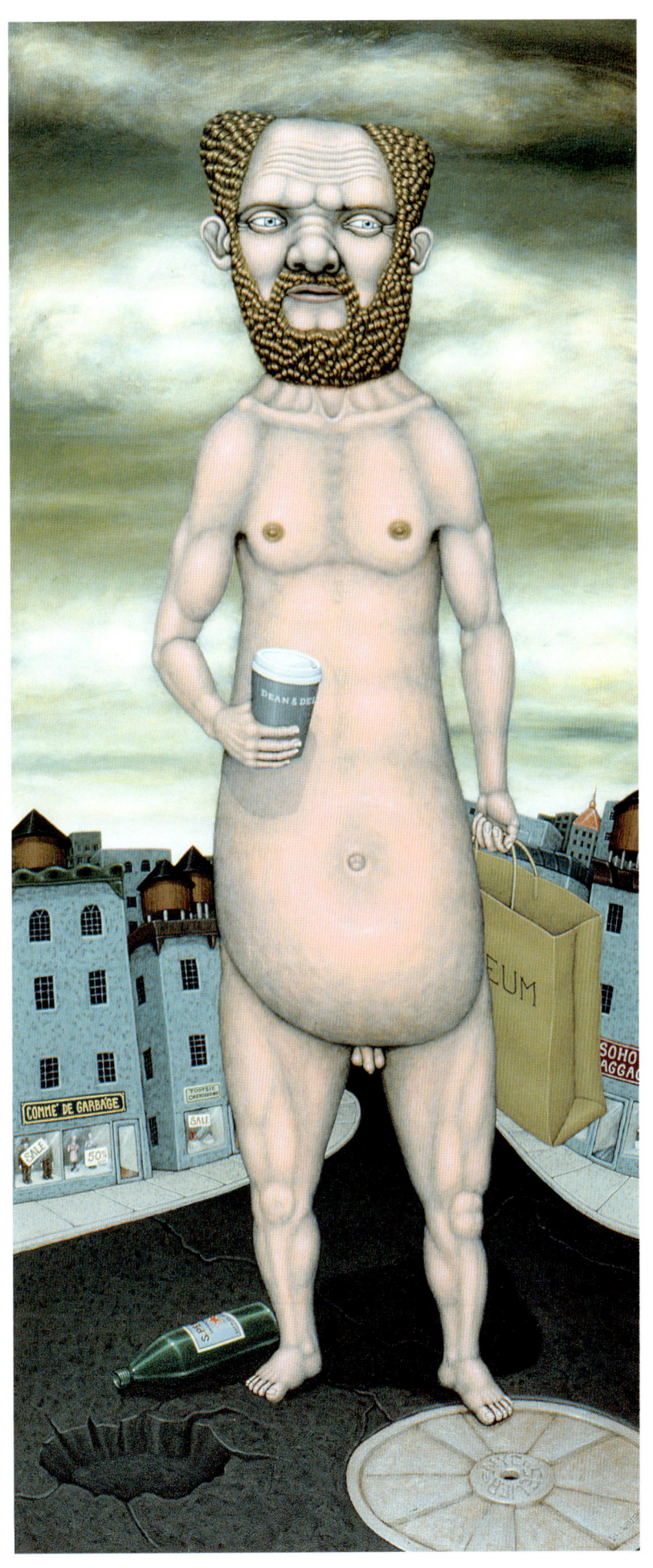

SOHO TOURIST
Acrylic on canvas
72" x 30"   1994
Collection of the artist

STUDY FOR BLUEBERRY PIE   Pencil   Actual size   Collection of the artist

The Fatties

FAT LADY WITH ICE CREAM   Acrylic on canvas   10" x 8"   1988   Collection Marjoe Gortner

FAT BLACK GUY #2   Acrylic on canvas   18" x 14"   1997   Collection of the artist

FAT LADY WITH DIET COKE   Acrylic on canvas   62" x 64"   1992   Collection of the artist

FAT LADY WITH BLUEBERRY PIE   Acrylic on canvas   18" x 14"   1990   Private collection

FAT LADY ON ECLAIRE   Acrylic on canvas   20" x 16"   1993   Collection Michael Young

FAT BLACK GUY #1   Acrylic on canvas   26" x 20"   1994   Collection Barry Goodman

FAT LADY WITH TREATS   Acrylic on canvas   18" x 14"   1988   Collection Kerstin Jamison

RED ALERT IN SUBURBIA   Acrylic on canvas   8" x 10"   2003   Collection of the artist

FAT LADY ATLAS   Acrylic on canvas   24" x 12"   1994   Collection of the artist

STUDY FOR CHICKEN HEAVEN IN HARLEM   Pencil   8" x 6"   2002   Collection of the artist

CHICKEN HEAVEN IN HARLEM Acrylic on canvas 38" x 32" 2003 Collection of the artist

WINNING ON WALL STREET   Acrylic on canvas   44" x 62"   1990   Collection Christopher Castroviejo

Business and Finance

DERANGED BUSINESSMAN   Acrylic on canvas   72" x 45"   1993   Collection Ross Burton

WALL STREET GAMBLER   Acrylic on canvas   64" x 42"   1994   Collection Marshall Auerbach

CRUCIFIXION ON WALL STREET   Acrylic on canvas   72" x 64"   1995   Collection Mark Davis

BUSINESSMAN WITH CIGAR   Acrylic on canvas   40" x 38"   1997   Collection of the artist

BUSINESSMAN IN HELL   Acrylic on canvas   20" x 16"   1996   Collection of the artist

CITY OF GOLD #2   Acrylic on canvas   18" x 14"   1992   Private Collection

THE RACE FOR DOLLARS   Acrylic on canvas   60" x 84"   1997   Collection of the artist

HUMAN SLOT MACHINE   Acrylic on canvas   46" x 32"   1990   Collection Christopher Castroviejo

WALL STREET MUMMY   Acrylic on canvas   40" x 34"   1996   Collection of the artist

MISTER AMERICA   Acrylic on canvas   64" x 42"   1995   Collection Lyle Hauser

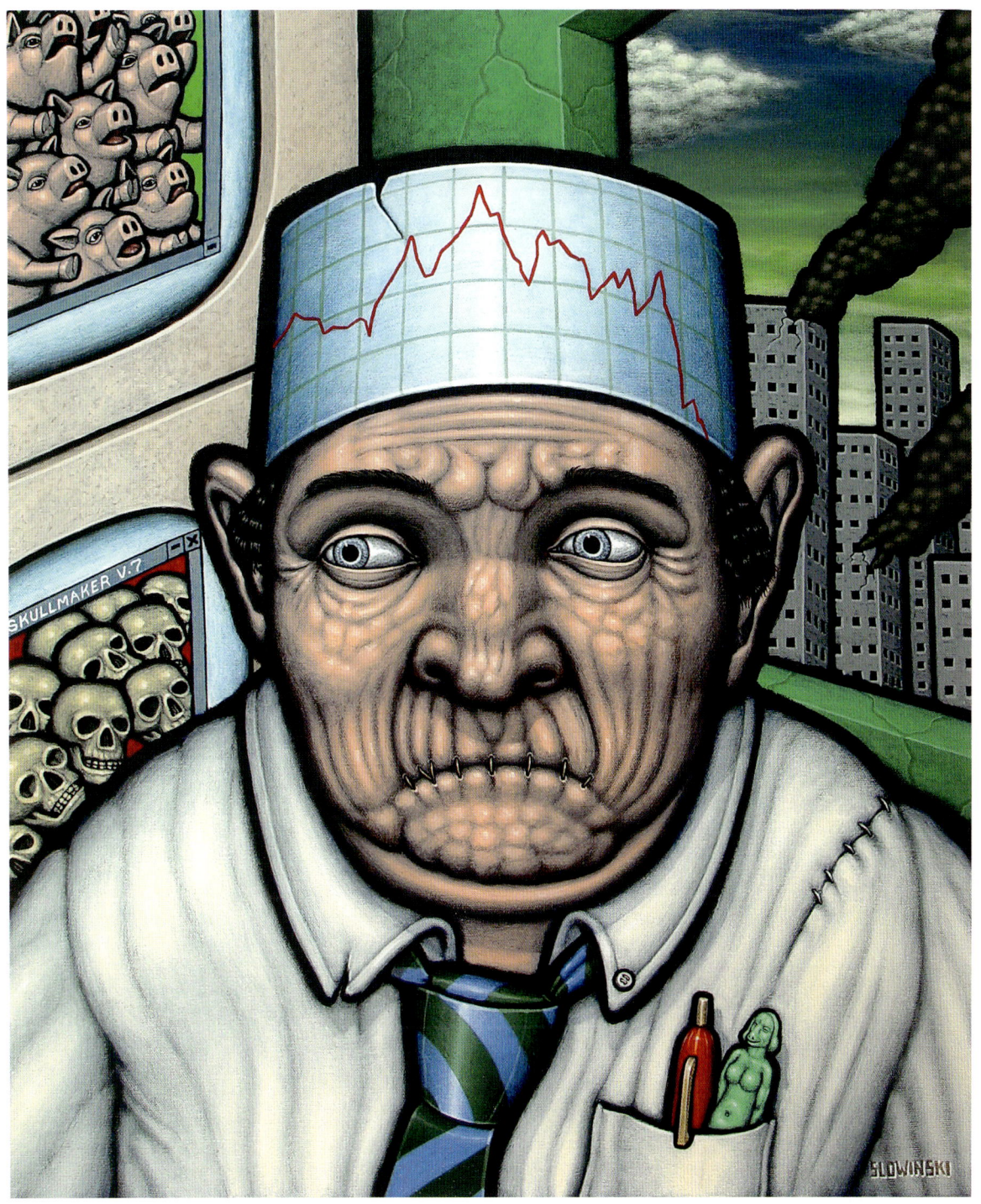

DEMISE OF WALL STREET   Acrylic on canvas   20" x 16"   2003   Collection of the artist

HELL   Pencil   8.5" x 8"   1992   Collection of the artist

Fire and Brimstone

BISHOP BIG NOSE   Acrylic on canvas   60" x 42"   1990   Collection Richard Golub

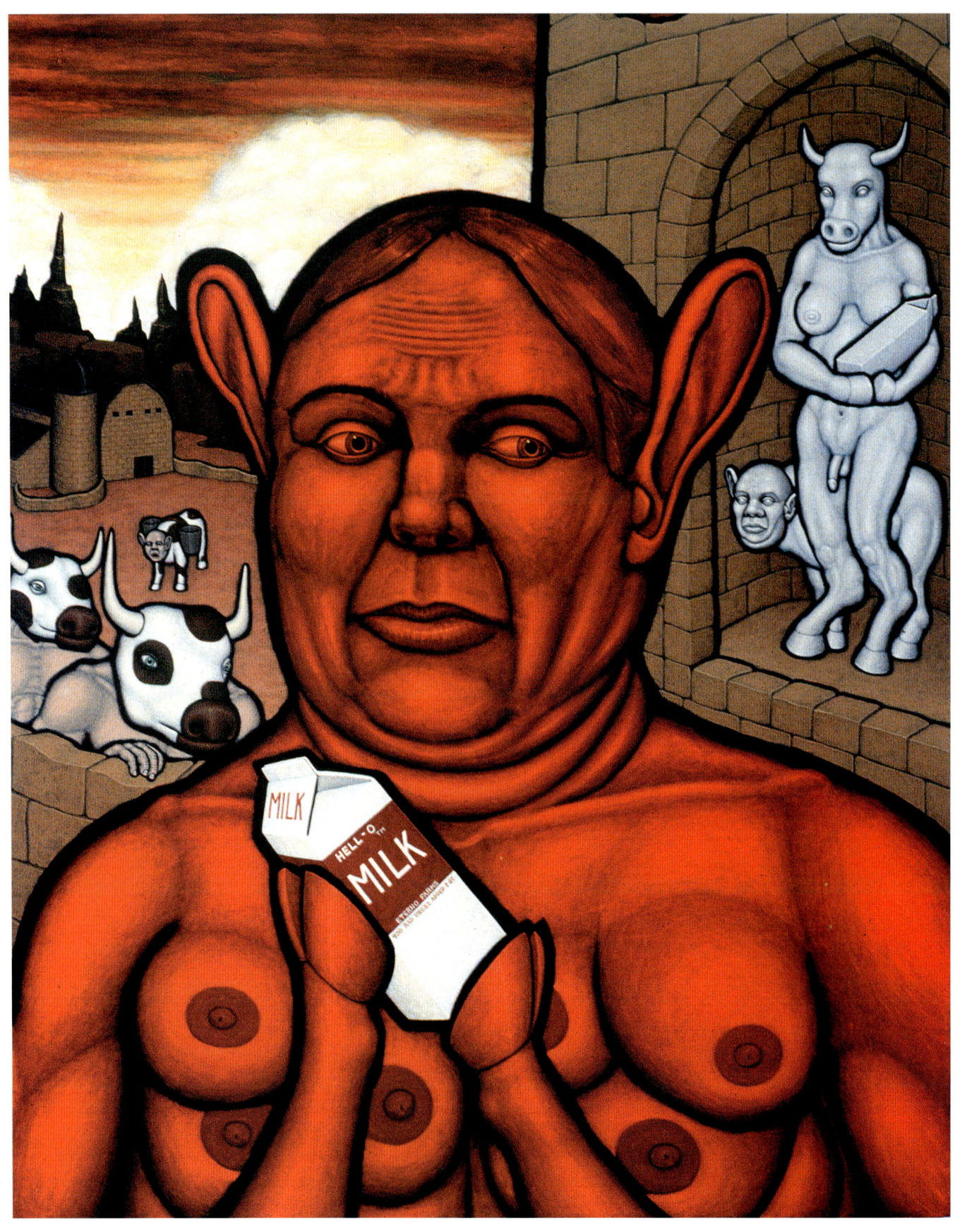

DEMON DAIRY   Acrylic on canvas   50" x 40"   1993   Collection of the artist

BOILING BUSINESSMAN   Acrylic on canvas   24" x 18"   1994   Collection Eric Sheer

WALK THROUGH TIME   Acrylic on canvas   78" x 52"   1993   Collection of the artist

TEMPTATION OF ST BOSCO   Acrylic on canvas   76" x 54"   1993   Collection of the artist

SUPPER AT EMMAUS   Acrylic on canvas   48" x 64"   2002   Collection of the artist

CRUNCHY BRAINS CEREAL   Acrylic on canvas   38" x 34"   2001   Collection of the artist

HELL FACTORY   Acrylic on canvas   48" x 64"   1989   Collection Marjoe Gortner

EASTER LUNCHEON AT THE RECTORY   Acrylic on canvas   56" x 42"   1988   Collection Barry Goodman

HOLY SMOKES   Acrylic on canvas   14" x 10"   1989   Private collection

Right: TEMPTATION OF ST ANTHONY
Acrylic on canvas   79" x 68"   1989
Collection Barry Goodman

HELL'S ROAD Acrylic on canvas 68" x 56" 1991 Collection Douglas Reymer

ROAD TO NOWHERE   Acrylic on canvas   48" x 64"   1991   Collection Barry Goodman

TEMPTATION OF ST AMERICANUS (prepatory drawing)   Pencil   18" x 12"   1990   Collection Orlando Lobello

TEMPTATION OF ST AMERICANUS   Acrylic on canvas   84" x 58"   1990   Collection Estate of Ted Churchill

NAPOLEON IN HELL (prepatory drawing)   Pencil   14" x 12"   1993   Collection of the artist

NAPOLEON IN HELL   Acrylic on canvas   24" x 22"   1993   Collection Ben Wood

DEMON NUN   Acrylic on canvas   62" x 64"   1991   Collection of the artist

PRAY   Acrylic on canvas   20" x 10"   2000   Collection of the artist

FRUITFACE MANDALLA (prepatory drawing)   Pencil   14" x 11"   1995   Collection Jeremy Eagle

FRUITFACE MANDALLA   Acrylic on canvas   60" x 48"   1995   Collection Tom Gleich

FRUITFACE   Acrylic on canvas   24" x 12"   1994   Collection of the artist

JELLY BEAN MAN   Acrylic on canvas   24" x 18"   1995   Collection Barry Goodman

HOME OWNER   Acrylic on canvas   12" x 9"   1985   Private Collection

An empire of unending horror- but funny
by Dakota Lane

Tim Slowinski's portraits, suburban scenes, evil icons and allegories defy easy categorization. Dealing with greed and corruption at a variety of levels, he draws us in through vividly painted raucous scenes. Nothing escapes his fictitious macro-lens: we zoom into situations of heightened paranoia and depravity, where absurdist humor fuses with an intense sense of horror.

His work bears comparison to a number of diverse painters and yet shuns any direct influence. Slowinski is in the avant-garde of the post-apocalyptic painters of the 21st century, finding an uneasy alliance with similarly dark art which depicts grim and lurid situations but falls short of his more fully realized vision. His work more aptly relates to the painters of centuries past.

Like a medieval moralist, he depicts a decadent pervasive evil—but instead of isolating it in a hellish realm, he pulls it straight out of America's heartland—its suburban homes, shopping centers and financial districts.

His clear, sophisticated palette, sense of detail and precise, translucent layers of paint are technically comparable to the masters. And yet his use of jet black outlines, which serve to underscore the simultaneous humor/horror effect, evoke a singular, strictly modern vision.

Slowinski's work appears as much influenced by the literary masters as by classic painters. His paintings of suburban families echo the bleak psychological landscapes and twisted humor of Kafka. Orwellian principles are manifest in

Slowinski's satirical contempt for hypocrisy, through his raw depictions of money brokers and use of farm animals as metaphoric stand-ins. His sharp, bitter humor and cheery, careening presentation serves to underscore his depiction of an empire of greed, bestial sexuality, over-mechanization and disconnected family.

It is fitting for an artist from the MTV era to create work that is not only filmic—(witness the vertiginous angles of careening grocery store aisles and suburban streets)—but video-evocative. The sudden flashes of movement, intense imagery and quick scenes are perfect food for a serotonin drained, attention deficit brain.

The subjects themselves convey the attributes of the TV addicted—whether victim or perpetrator, they portray a traumatized, jangled persona: women with shell-shocked eyes engaging in automatic pilot activities, a series of suburban "blockheads" who like automatons are heading out into the world of daily business. Each painting an eerie gift from a seamless and continuous world. He achieves this through acute and painstaking precision, sparing no care with the homeliest detail.

Every scene feels connected to an even more seriously unhinged world and he provides those connections through depth of perspective. The vanishing point never quite vanishes; there is no respite to be found even in a sunset. If the central image is perverse, the peripheral images are even more so—he uses the periphery of the canvas to create a mounting, Hitchcockian sense of paranoia. Little catastrophic scenarios are often unfolding just at the very edge of our vision.

Alternately, he devises a pocket of placidity so calm as to be deranged—utterly still buildings, spotless streets, perfectly groomed lawns seem to be the breeding grounds for untold acts of aberrance. His work is nothing if not relentless; every aspect conspires to create no exit from the house of horror called daily existence. Even the domestic details are unsettling, things look like they are about to crawl out of the perfectly aligned cereal boxes and they often do.

The nobility of mankind is present only by its absence from his work; further dehumanization is represented through people being fused with animals, crossbred with machines, entrapped within a labyrinth of technological tortures. In one comic and viscerally disturbing portrait, a man is fashioned entirely out of gold coins.

Slowinski touches on the robotic nature of modern humans. We rarely see a flicker of sensitivity or choice in his subject's eyes. With the detachment of a surgeon, he explores the subtleties of flesh, from its variant subtle tones to the way it drapes over sinews and muscles. He depicts grand obese people not only to represent the ugly American, but to indulge his love of form.

Although race sometimes seems incidental in his paintings (the obese African American man in *Fat Black Man* could just as easily be white)—it is more often a conscious choice, used as way to bring home man's acts of injustice and violence. In *Dearth of a Nation* and *Chicken Heaven in Harlem* depictions of rape condemn centuries of racial and economic slavery.

His subjects are lonely to the point of pathology—the sense of alienation is acute, acts of physical intimacy are brutal (*The Rape of Gumby*, *Nazi Medical Experiment*)—even the members of his "Psychedelic Family" triptych are painted alone. In *Dysfunctional Family*, he offers a portrait of literal enmeshment—body parts of various family members are knotted together, arms becoming tentacles, intertwined and entangled, a quiet yet palpable hysteria simmering beneath the placid facade of every person.

The emotions of Slowinski's subjects are often underplayed. The suburban mothers tend to wear frozen masks of stoic calm; victims of various tortures have a chilling sense of complacency, sometimes infused with anguish that cloud their eyes like those of sainted martyrs.

Slowinski's mordant wit and fatalistic humor serve to cut through the niceties like a laser. Apart from his generous gifts as a painter, the strength of his work is derived from his honesty; his unflinching reiteration of his vision of modern America provides us with a mirror that may be less distorted than we wish.

Dakota Lane is an author and art critic.
dakota@netstep.net

EVOLUTION OF MAN   Acrylic on canvas   12" x 16"   1996   Collection Arnie Weissman

Creation and Evolution

FUTURE MAN   Acrylic on canvas   18" x 14"   1999   Collection of the artist

THE GARDEN OF EDEN
Acrylic on canvas
90" x 48"   1990
Private Collection

DOG   Acrylic on canvas   20" x 16"   1998   Collection of the artist

Animals and Farm

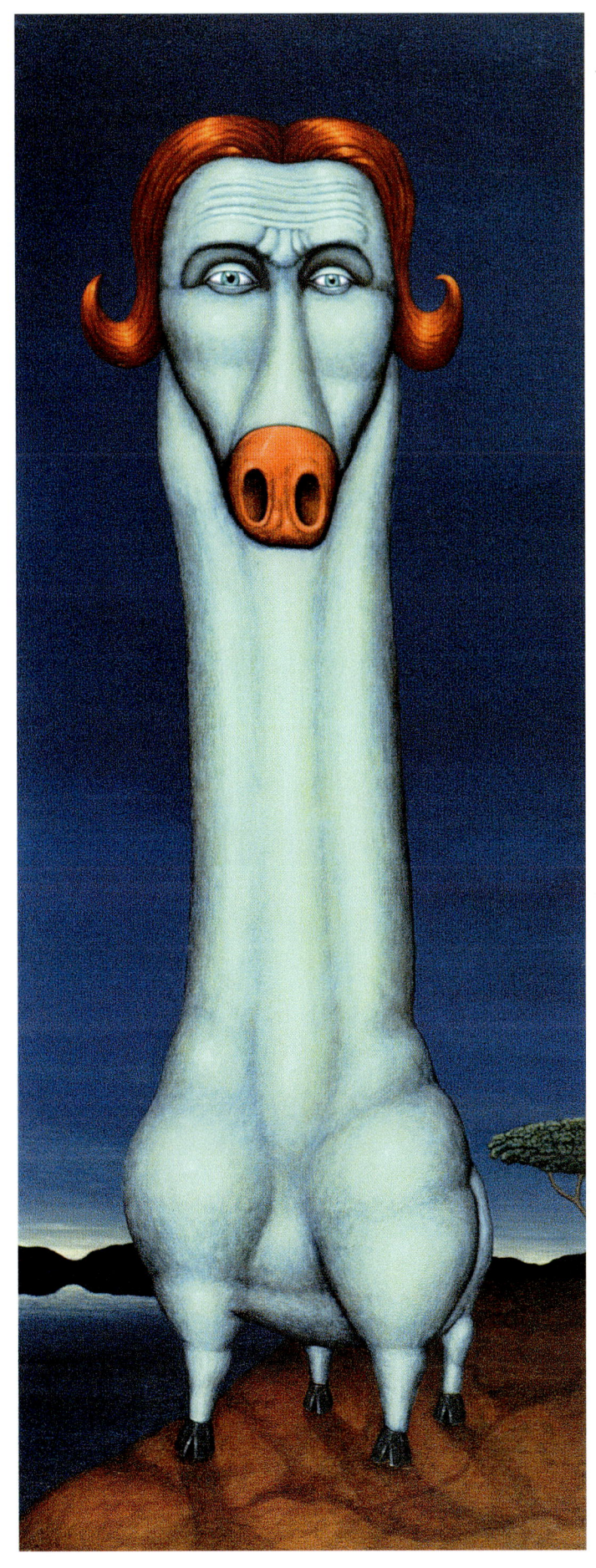

PENISAURUS
Acrylic on canvas
48" x 18"   1993
Collection Wolfgang Birk
 Dominique Joseph

111

TURTLE   Acrylic on canvas   8" x 10"   1999   Collection EJ Robinson

PIG   Acrylic on canvas   10" x 8"   1994   Private Collection

DOG RIDE (prepatory drawing) Pencil 12" x 11" 1992 Collection of the artist

DOG RIDE #2   Acrylic on canvas   72" x 64"   1992   Collection of the artist

DOGRIDE   Acrylic on canvas   12" x 9"   1988   Collection Joel Cooper

HORSE Acrylic on canvas 10" x 8" 1995 Collection Kit Lee

MAD COW   Acrylic on canvas   24" x 12"   2002   Collection of the artist

MONSANTO'S CURSE   Acrylic on canvas   72" x 64"   2000   Collection of the artist

COPULATING PIGS   Acrylic on canvas   6" x 8"   2002   Collection Chris Nowlan

SCARECROW   Acrylic on canvas   56" x 42"   1985   Collection Susan Wexner

PORK WAGON   Acrylic on canvas   18" x 14"   1989   Private Collection

Food

EGG WAGON   Acrylic on canvas   18" x 14"   1989   Collection Christine Jamison

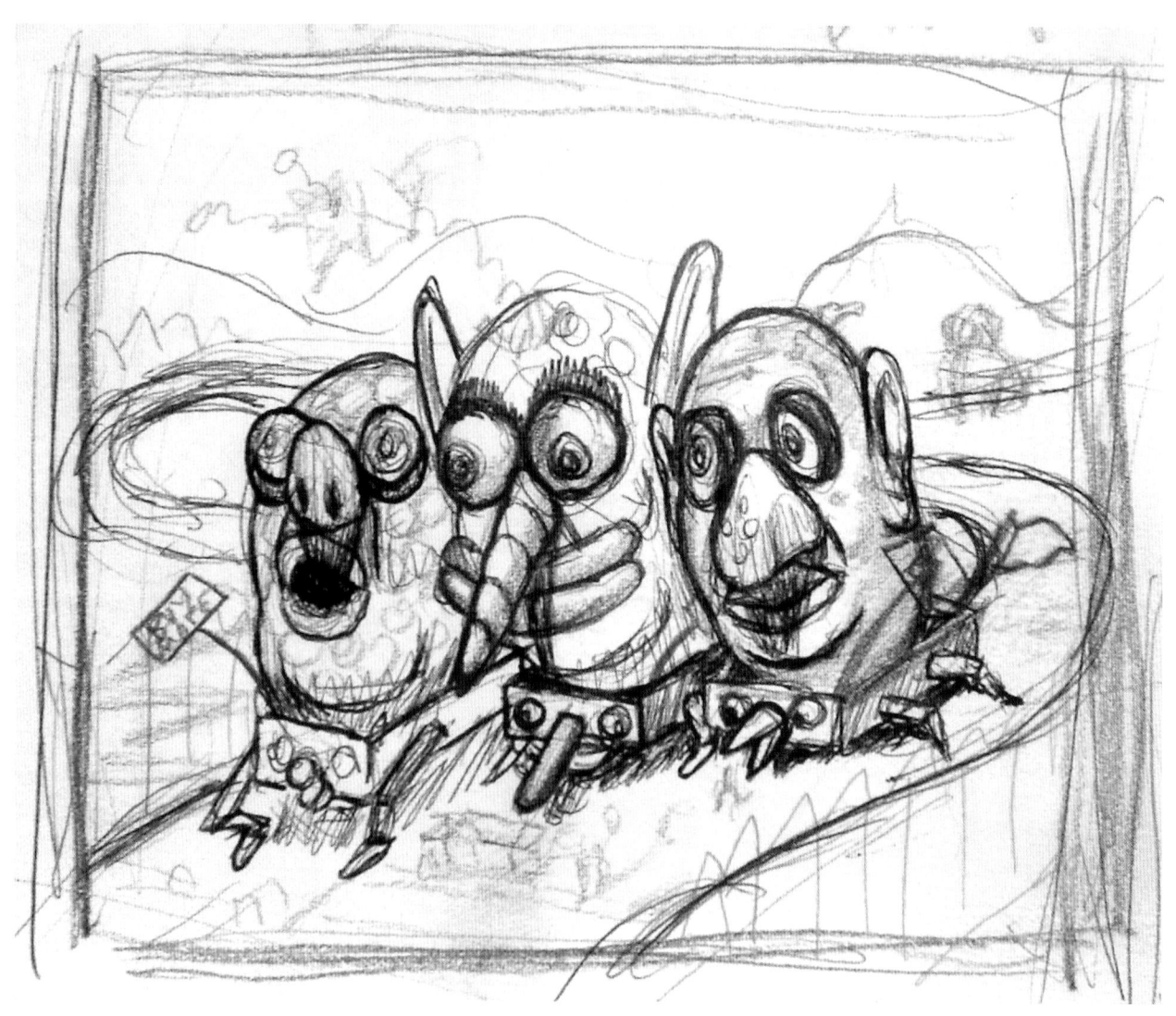

PROMOTIONAL VEHICLES   Pencil   4" x 5"   1990   Collection of the artist

MEAT PROMOTIONAL VEHICLE   Acrylic on canvas   12" x 10"   1989   Collection Norman Holden

ST THERESA TAKES A HOLIDAY   Pencil   8" x 6"   1991   Collection of the artist

WINE TASTING   Acrylic on canvas   68" x 72"   1991   Collection Barry Goodman

FRUITWAGON   Acrylic on canvas   18" x 14"   1991   Collection Julie Pacer

ALIENS WITH TV DINNER Acrylic on canvas 18" x 14" 1992 Collection David Shapiro

MOBY'S PIZZA   Acrylic on canvas   52" x 56"   1988   Collection Charles and Judy Gartman

CHICKEN HEAVEN   Acrylic on canvas   76" x 64"   1987   Collection of the artist

POTATO EATER   Acrylic on canvas   30" x 20"   1993   Collection Joseph and Gertrude Slowinski

EGGY   Acrylic on canvas   56" x 42"   1993   Collection Alan and Cecelia Brehm

CARROT NOSE CLOWN   Acrylic on canvas   38" x 32"   1992   Collection of the artist

Clowns and Freaks

MISS TINY   Pencil   12" x 10"   1987   Collection Leonard Freid

CARROT NOSE CLOWN   Acrylic on canvas
14" x 10"   1986   Collection Estate of Sam Klein

FAT MAN CLOWN   Acrylic on canvas
12" x 10"   1986   Collection Estate of Sam Klein

135

HEROIC MAN Acrylic on canvas 38" x 32" 1996 Collection of the artist

ALIEN FEMALE   Acrylic on canvas   58" x 42"   1995   Collection of the artist

SHIT HEAD   Acrylic on canvas   10" x 8"   1994   Collection Wolfgang Birk, Dominique Joseph

Rogue Heads

MENTAL CASE   Acrylic on canvas   10" x 8"   1994   Private collection

DUMMY   Acrylic on canvas   10" x 8"   1994   Private collection

MEAT HEAD   Acrylic on canvas   10" x 8"   1994   Collection Sam Whitman

AIR HEAD   Acrylic on canvas   10" x 8"   1994   Collection Richard Golub

FAT HEAD   Acrylic on canvas   10" x 8"   1994   Collection Paul Benson

HOT HEAD   Acrylic on canvas   10" x 8"   1994   Collection Barry Goodman

FISH FACE   Acrylic on canvas   10" x 8"   1994   Collection Jill Strauss

DICK HEAD   Acrylic on canvas   10" x 8"   1994   Collection Richard Golub

POT HEAD   Acrylic on canvas   10" x 8"   1994   Collection Janet Hoffman

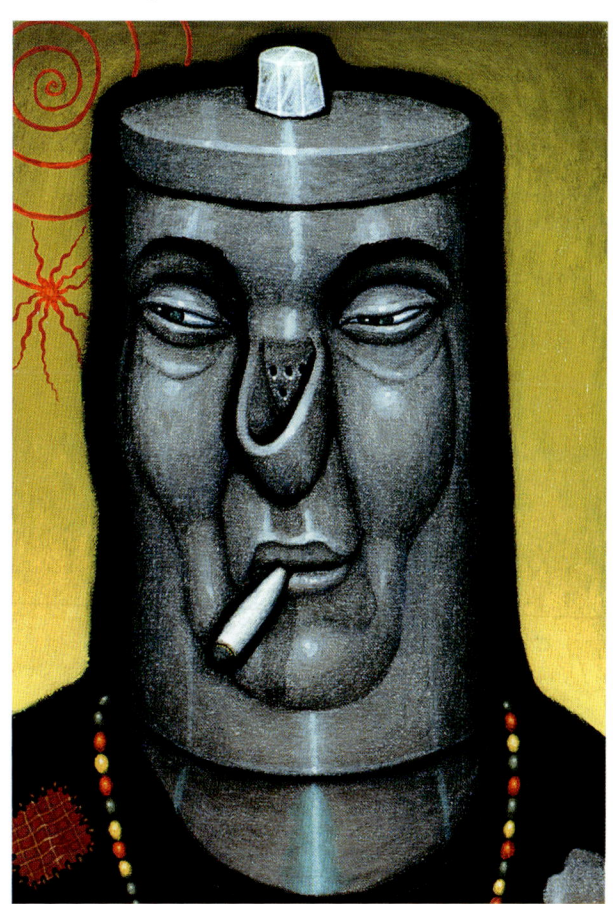

BLUES MAN   Acrylic on canvas   72" x 46"   2000   Collection of the artist

YELLOW FACE   Acrylic on canvas   72" x 46"   2000   Collection of the artist

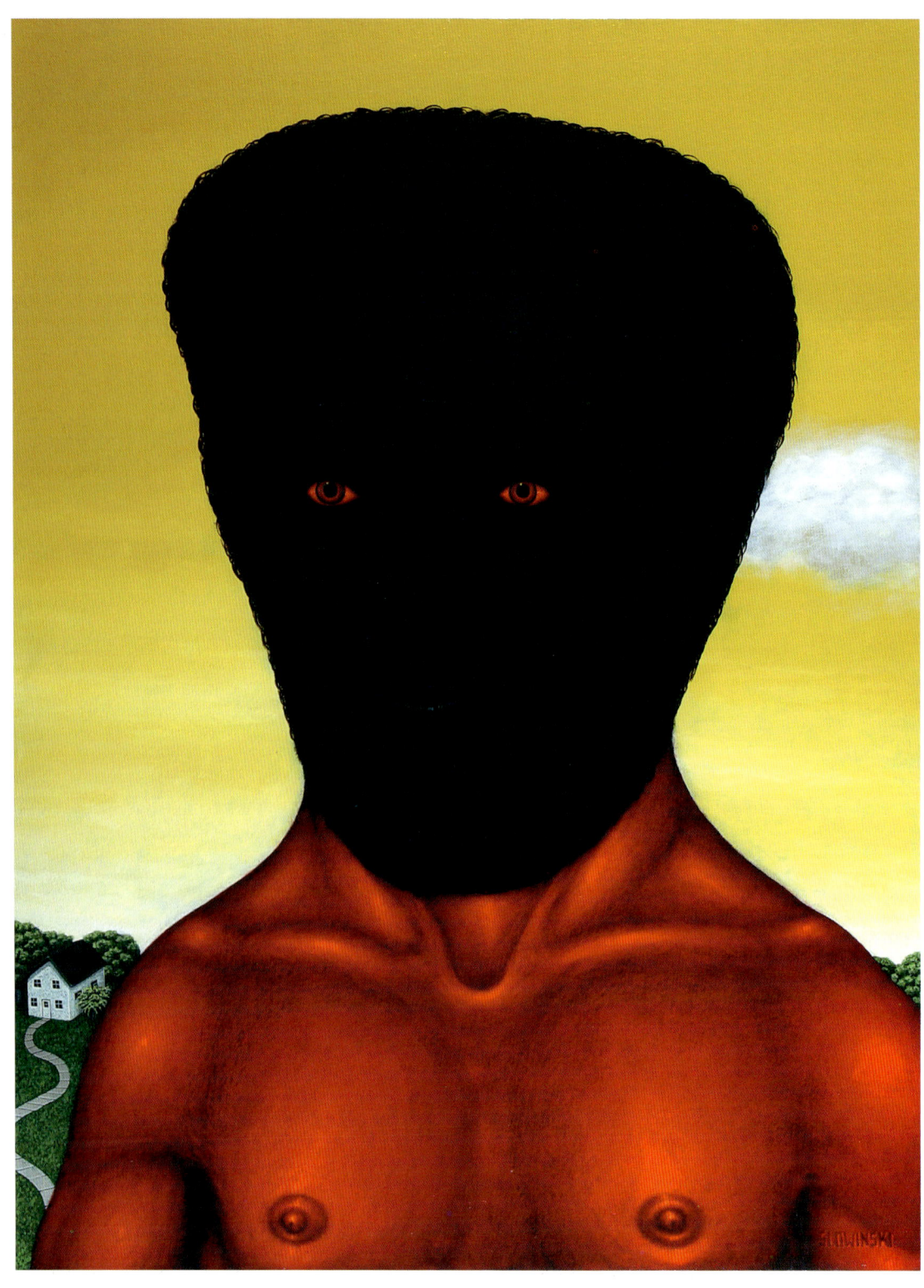

BLACK FACE   Acrylic on canvas   44" x 32"   2001   Collection of the artist

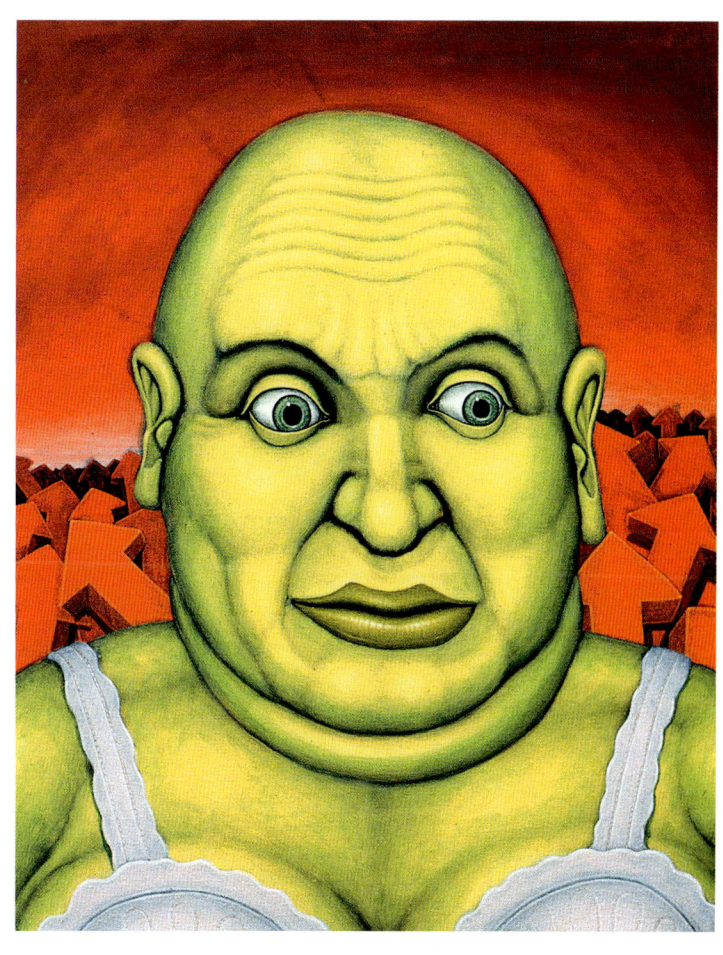

PICKLE HEAD   Acrylic on canvas   18" x 14"   1993   Collection of the artist

NUMBER HEAD   Acrylic on canvas   18" x 14"   1993   Collection of the artist

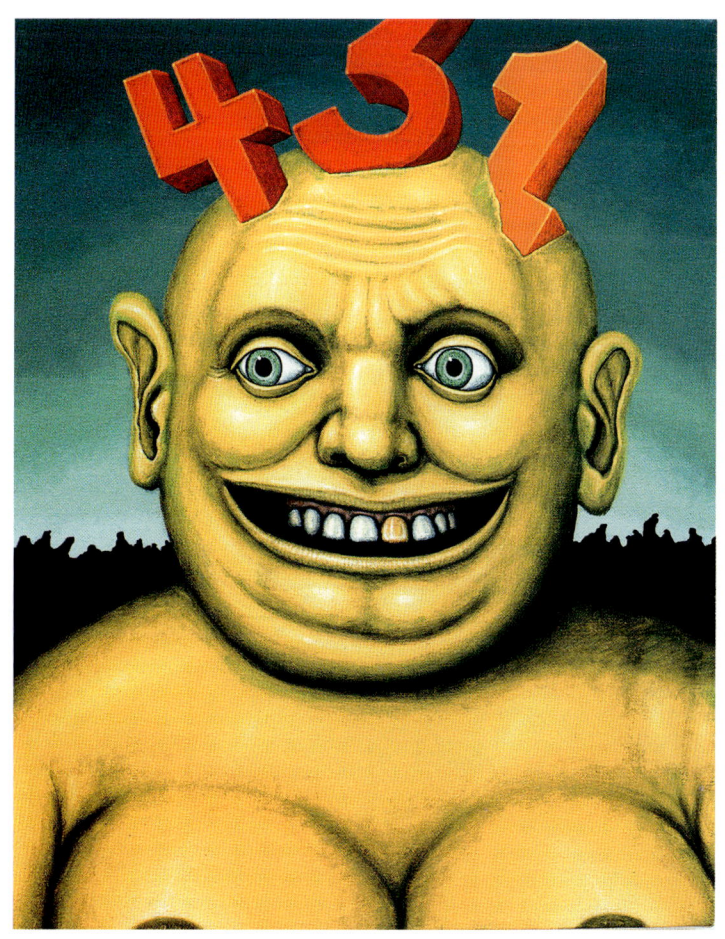

HALLOWEEN PARTY IN WASHINGTON DC   Acrylic on canvas   14" x 18"   1990   Collection of the artist

Parties and Politics

UNCLE FRANK   Acrylic on canvas   14" x 9"   1991   Collection Cindy Lee

TWO FACE Acrylic on canvas 46" x 32" 1996 Collection of the artist

SLUT-O FOR PRESIDENT   Acrylic on canvas   18" x 14"   1992   Collection of the artist

ELECTION DAY PARADE   Acrylic on canvas   18" x 14"   1988   Collection Leonard Freid

ESCAPE FROM TOYTOWN Acrylic on canvas 78" x 68" 1989 Collection Estate of Ted Churchill

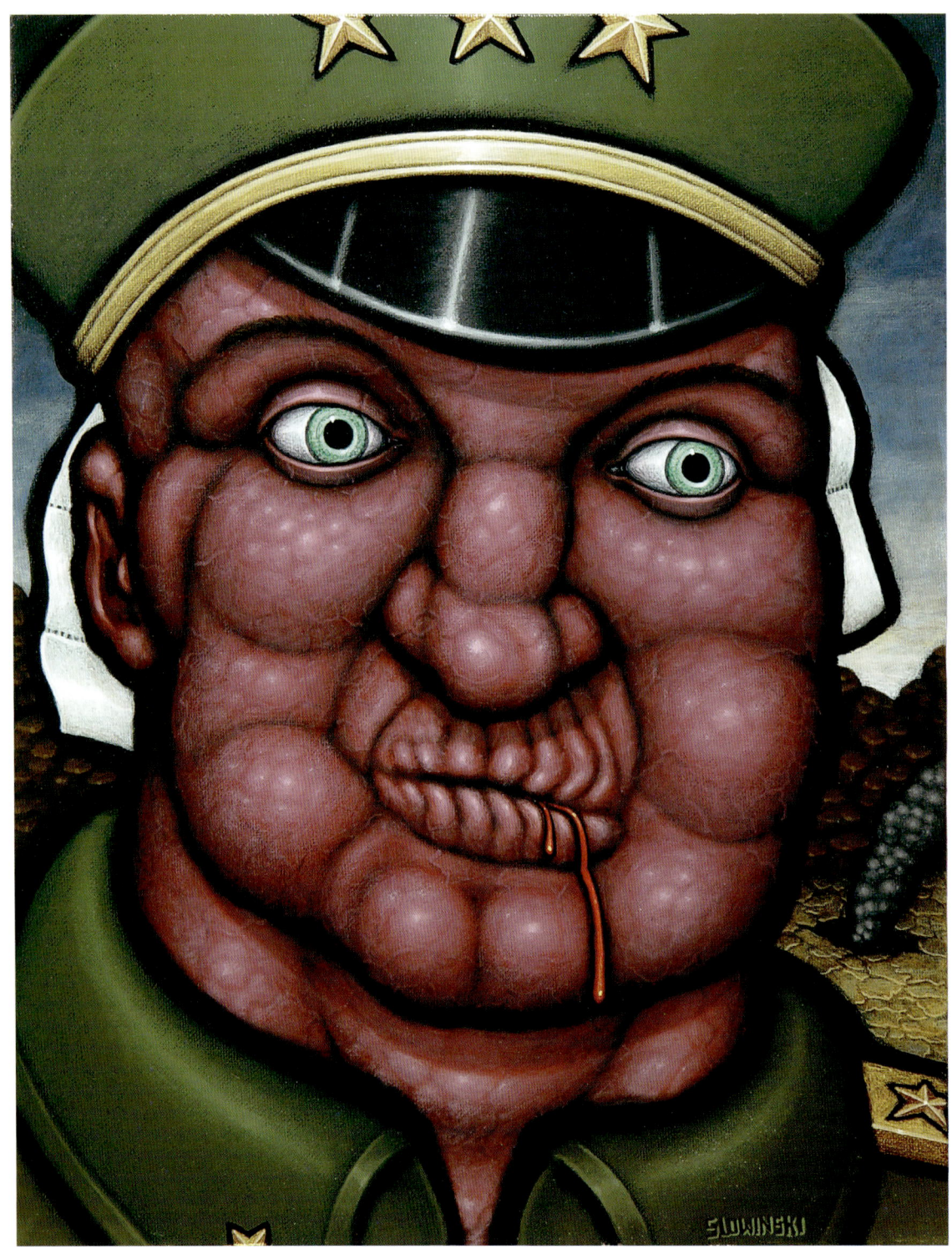

GENERAL COLON BOWEL   Acrylic on canvas   16" x 12"   2003   Collection of the artist

UNCLE FRANK'S WAR DANCE Acrylic on canvas 24" x 18" 2003 Collection of the artist

SKETCH FOR COURTROOM DRAMA   Pencil   14" x 11"   1993   Collection of the artist

COURTROOM DRAMA   Acrylic on canvas   48" x 84"   1996   Collection Ross Berton

NAZI MEDICAL EXPERIMENT   Pencil   18" x 14"   1998   Collection Barry Goodman

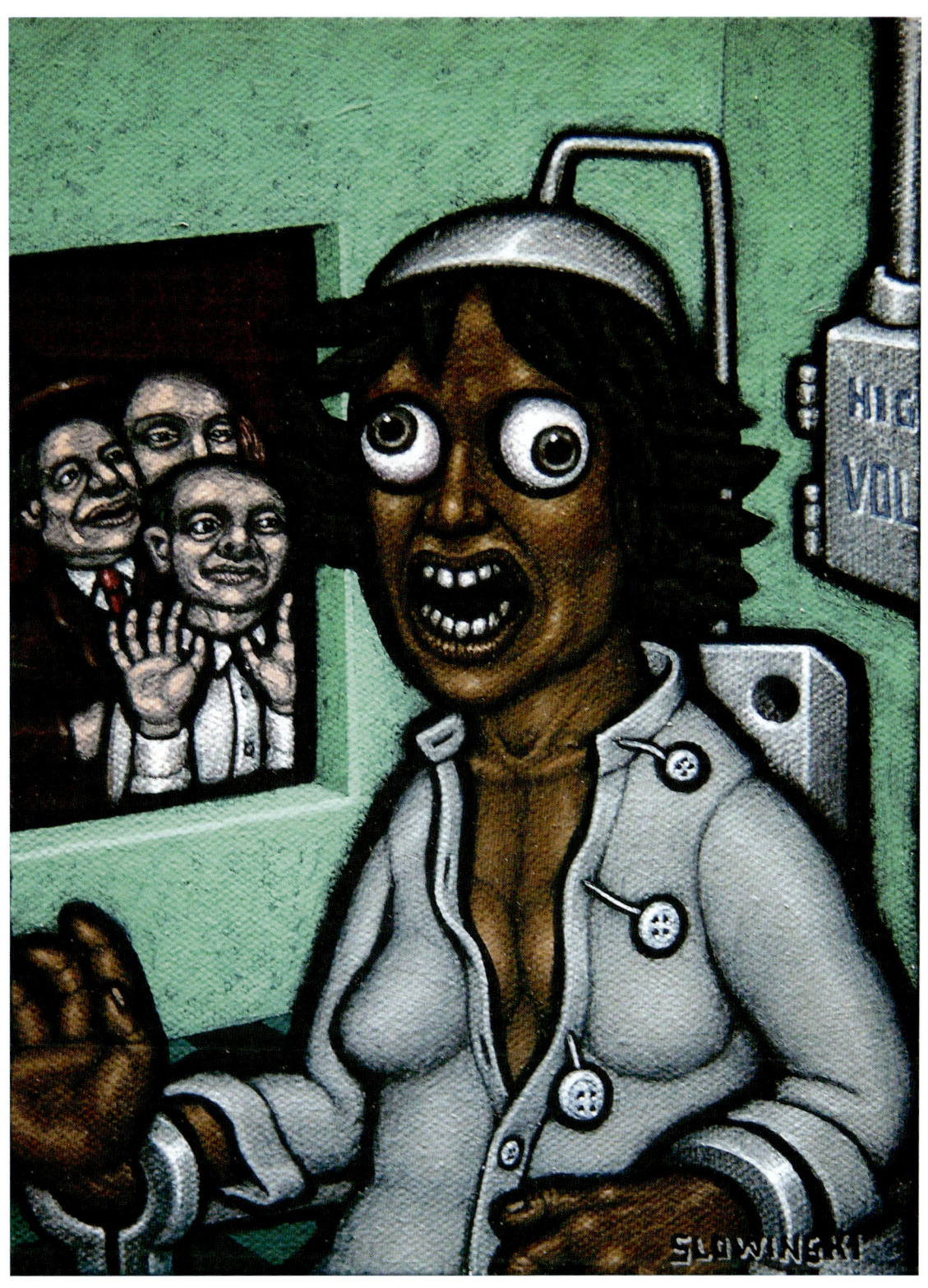

VICTIM   Acrylic on canvas   11" x 8"   1998   Collection EJ Robinson

SNAP, CRACKLE AND POP   Acrylic on canvas   72" x 62"   1991   Collection Bob and Karen Gerstl

Cultural Icons

CAPTAIN CRUNCH   Acrylic on canvas   94" x 52"   1990   Collection Richard Golub

THEY FINALLY LEAVE TOWN   Acrylic on canvas   72" x 54"   1986   Collection Ken Silva

SUNMAID   Acrylic on canvas   18" x 14"   1991   Collection Alan and Cecelia Brehm

DEARTH OF A NATION   Acrylic on canvas   78" x 66"   2000   Collection of the artist

SHIP OF FOOLS   Acrylic on canvas   60" x 44"   1995   Collection of the artist

THE RAPE OF GUMBY   Acrylic on canvas   72" x 48"   2000   Collection of the artist

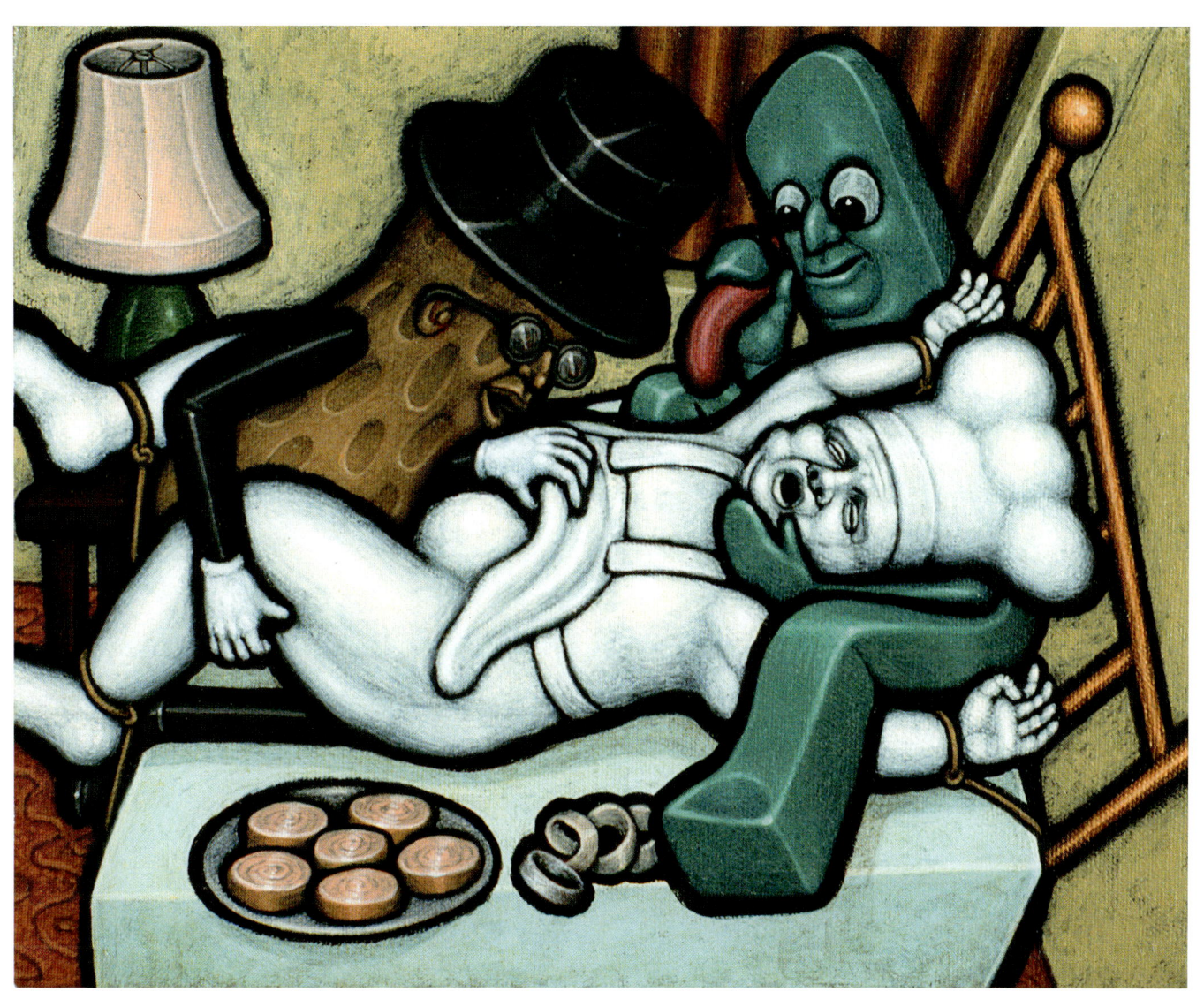

GUMBY'S REVENGE   Acrylic on canvas   8" x 10"   1999   Collection Barry Goodman

ARAB WITH COLA   Acrylic on canvas   6" x 4"   1988   Collection Richard Golub

Consumerism

SHOP-A-MATIC   Acrylic on canvas   24" x 18"   2000   Collection Steve Pastore

SMOKE REDMAN   Acrylic on canvas   14" x 10"   1989   Collection Jorge Letelier Yavar

HOLY SMOKES Acrylic on canvas 12" x 10" 1988 Collection Richard Golub

CHINAMAN WITH YOO HOO   Acrylic on canvas   6" x 4"   1995   Private collection

ARAB WITH CAMELS   Acrylic on canvas   6" x 4"   1995   Private collection

SACRED VOW CAT FOOD   Acrylic on canvas   10" x 8"   1989   Collection Richard Golub

ARABS WITH FRUITY SODAS   Acrylic on canvas   16" x 20"   1989   Collection Kerstin Jamison

OPERATION DIE HARD (prepatory drawing) Pencil 10" x 12" 2001 Collection of the artist

Doctors and Nurses

OPERATION DIE HARD   Acrylic on canvas   68" x 84"   2002   Collection of the artist

GIANTNOSEITIS   Acrylic on canvas   18" x 14"   1994   Collection of the artist

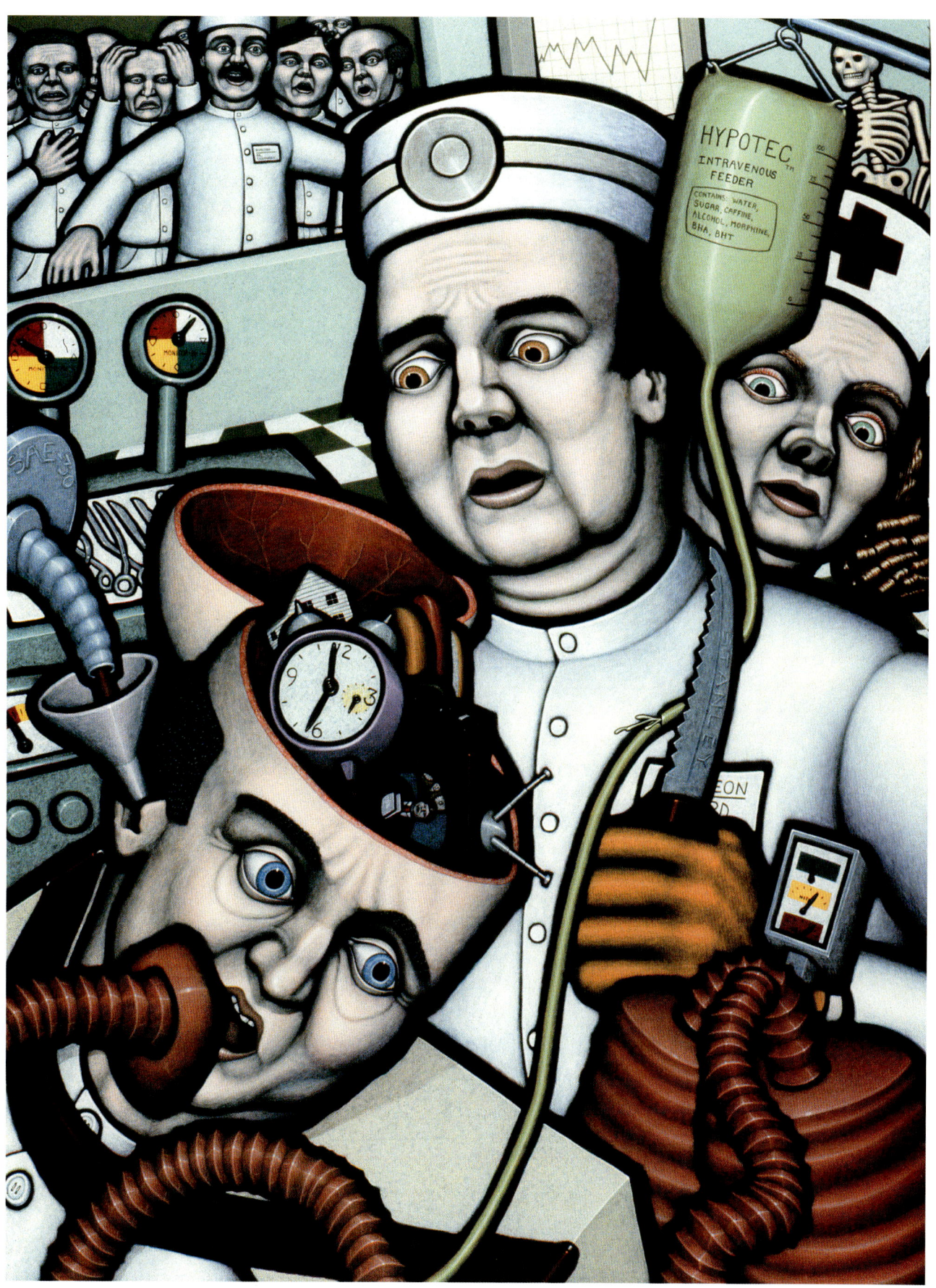

BRAIN SURGERY   Acrylic on canvas   56" x 42"   1990   Collection Daryl Isaacs MD

OPERATION   Acrylic on canvas   18" x 14"   1993   Collection Wolfgang Birk / Dominique Joseph

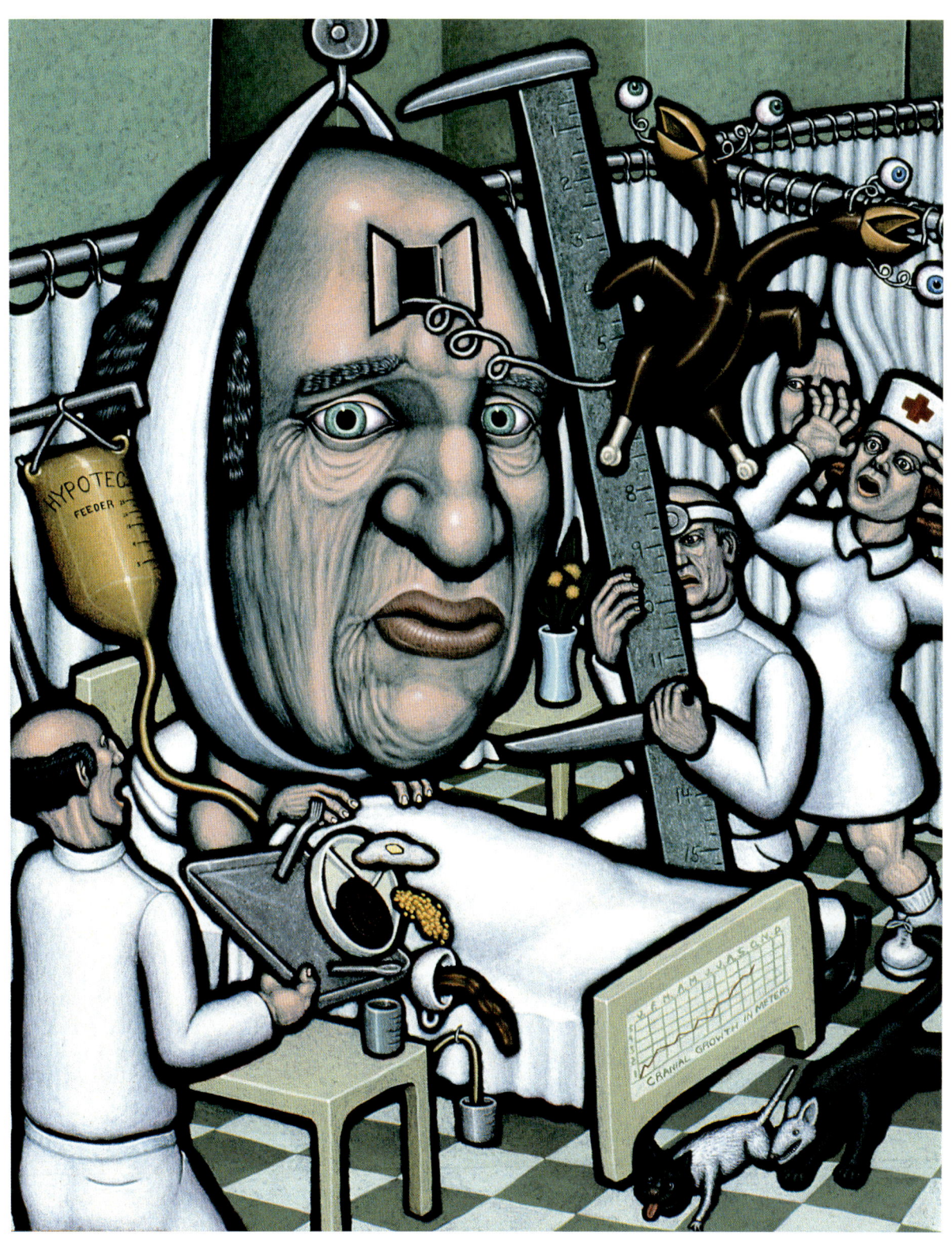

GIANTNOSEITIS   Acrylic on canvas   18" x 14"   1990   Collection Christine Jamison

RIVER OF SLIME   Acrylic on canvas   32" x 38"   1988   Collection Pascal Jeandet

Industrial Nightmare

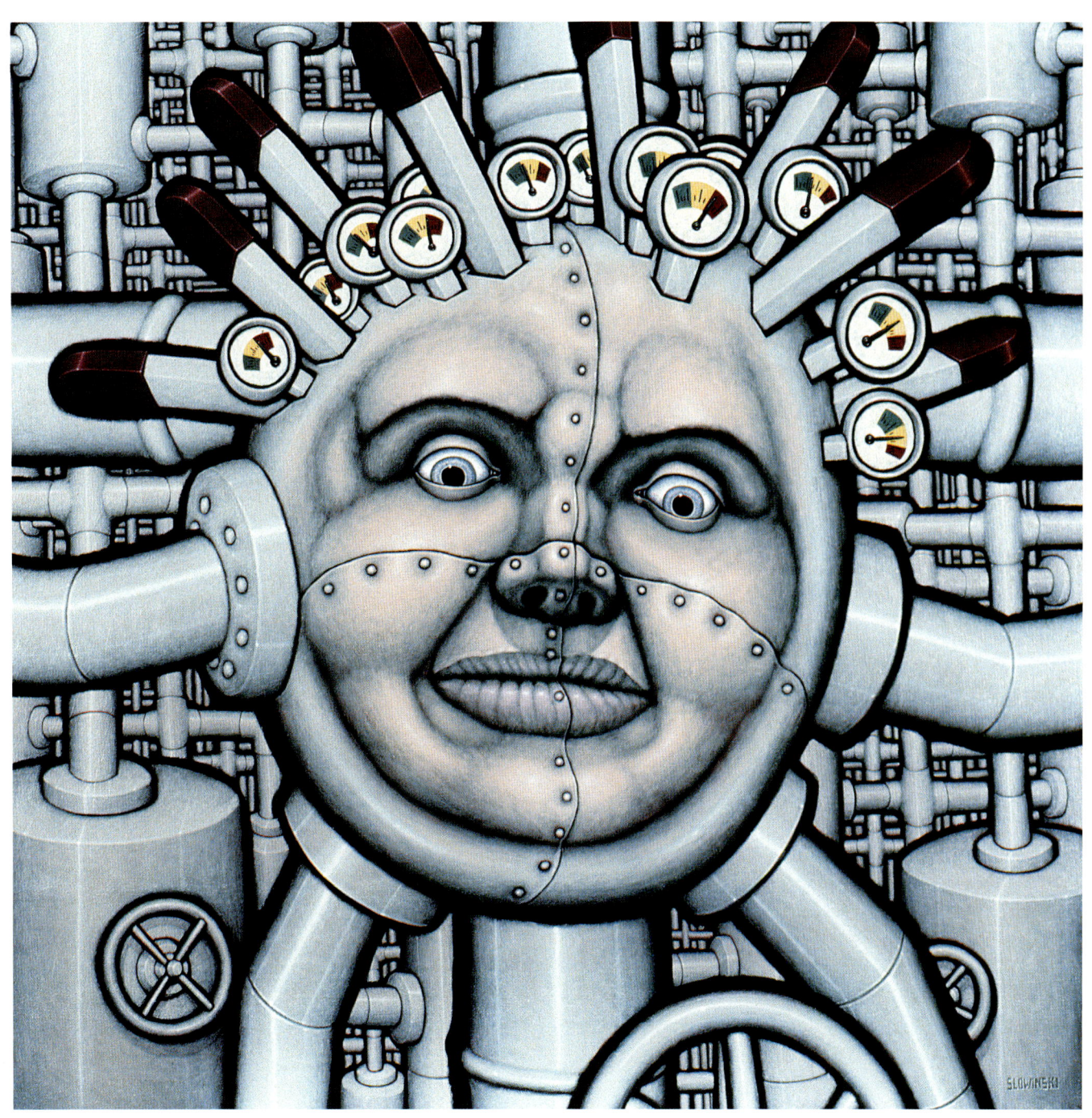

HEAD OF INDUSTRY #3   Acrylic on canvas   45" x 46"   1996   Collection of the artist

TAR HEAD   Acrylic on canvas   46" x 32"   1995   Collection Ross Berton

EXPLODING HEAD   Acrylic on canvas   56" x 42"   1993   Collection Lyle Hauser

SOCIAL SUICIDE (prepatory drawing)   Pencil   12" x 12"   2001   Collection of the artist

SOCIAL SUICIDE   Acrylic on canvas   64" x 44"   2001   Collection of the artist